DEM●S

Demos is an independent think-tank committed to radical thinking on the long-term problems facing the UK and other advanced industrial societies.

It aims to develop the ideas – both theoretical and practical – that will help to shape the politics of the 21st century, and to improve the breadth and quality of political debate.

Demos publishes books and a quarterly journal and undertakes substantial empirical and policy-oriented research projects. Demos is a registered charity.

In all its work Demos brings together people from a wide range of backgrounds in business, academia, government, the voluntary sector and the media to share and cross-fertilise ideas and experiences.

For further information and
subscription details please write to:
Demos
9 Bridewell Place
London, EC4V 6AP
Telephone: 0171 353 4479
Facsimile: 0171 353 4481
email: joanna@demos.demon.co.uk

After Social Democracy:

Politics, capitalism and the common life

John Gray

First published in 1996 by
Demos
9 Bridewell Place
London EC4V 6AP
Telephone: 0171 353 4479
Facsimile: 0171 353 4481
e-mail: joanna@demos.demon.co.uk
© Demos 1996

Paper No. 18
ISBN 1 898309 52 3
Printed in Great Britain by
EG Bond Ltd
Designed by Esterson Lackersteen
Thanks to Adrian Taylor

Contents

Introduction **7**

Where we are now **10**

What social democracy was **24**

Right, left and globalisation **29**

The diversity of market institutions **34**

Welfare, local justice and complex fairness **41**

What we can hope for **56**

Notes **59**

Acknowledgements

Many people have helped me distil my thoughts on the issues addressed in this paper. I wish to thank the participants in a small intensive seminar at Demos at which an early sketch of this paper was given a critical airing. Comments by Tony Giddens and David Miliband were particularly helpful. Conversations with Will Hutton, Raymond Plant, Robert Skidelsky and George Walden have advanced my thinking on several questions discussed in the paper. Geoff Mulgan's comments and thoughts have been invaluable.

Introduction

This paper has been written to be entirely freestanding and fully accessible to the reader in its own terms. But it can also be read as the third in a trio of papers, the first of which is *The moral foundations of market institutions*, published by the Institute of Economic Affairs in 1992 and republished as chapter two of my book, *Beyond the New Right: market, government and the common environment*, Routledge, 1993, and the second of which was *The undoing of conservatism*, published in 1994 by the Social Market Foundation and republished as chapter six of my book, *Enlightenment's wake: politics and culture at the close of the modern age*, Routledge, 1995.

Like the two earlier papers, this Demos paper reflects my conviction that the established traditions of British political thought; liberal, conservative, and socialist, cannot meet the challenges posed by the technological and cultural environment of Britain in the late modern period. New thought is needed, in which debts to the past are light.

The object of this essay is to break new ground. Its starting point is the belief that, though the emerging social-democratic consensus in Britain represents a considerable advance on the formulaic debates of the New

Right and the Old Left, it nevertheless embodies assumptions and modes of thought that belong to an historical context that has vanished beyond recovery. That context has been destroyed partly by neoliberal policy, and, more importantly, by global economic and technological developments. The risk is that, as policy framed in terms of social-democratic ideas proves to lack leverage on the dangers and social costs associated with these developments, atavistic and antiliberal positions on both Left and Right will enjoy a new lease of life.

This essay is a modest effort to prepare for that eventuality. It is a study neither in political philosophy nor in public policy, but something in between. It is an exercise in what might be called mid-level theorising; an attempt to illuminate the historical context in which we find ourselves, to identify its constraints and possibilities, and to consider the political responses they evoke. I argue that:

- the historical context in which social-democratic conceptions made sense has ceased to exist;
- a communitarian liberal perspective is a natural successor both to neoliberalism and social democracy;
- and that the social-democratic commitment to egalitarian principles must be abandoned and replaced by concern for norms of fairness which are local, in that they dictate different distributions of goods in different contexts or domains, according to the shared social understanding we have of these goods.

For example, there is every reason why educational practice should on the whole be meritocratic and the allocation of medical care determined by judgments of need. Neither the neoliberal reverence for the cash nexus nor social-democratic ideals of overall equality do justice to notions of local fairness which animate the common culture. Equally, neither the fundamentalist project of the New Right in seeking to revive vanished forms of family life, nor the standard liberal, libertarian and social-democratic position that the state and public policy should be silent or neutral on all issues to do with the institution of the family, accords with the needs of the varieties of families our society harbours. All these doctrinal positions are far from ordinary experience, in which people who are used to making their own choices are constantly improvising on the forms of life they have inherited. The central claim of the communitarian liberal perspective is that individual choices will not issue in flourishing human lives unless they occur in the context of common forms of life that are rich in options.

None of the people who have assisted me with this paper will agree with all of what I have to say in it; some will dissent strongly from parts of it. Accordingly, none of them shares with me responsibility for any of it, which remains mine alone.

John Gray
Jesus College, Oxford
January 1996

Where we are now

Social democrats have failed to perceive that Thatcherism was a modernising project with profound and irreversible consequences for political life in Britain. The question cannot now be: how are the remains of social democracy to be salvaged from the ruins of Thatcherism? but instead: what is Thatcherism's successor?

Like the wet Tories, social democrats did not grasp the radicalism of the Thatcher project in sweeping away old class deferences and hierarchies. Many of them still view it as a blip on the screen of history, to be followed by a return to the 'normal politics' of pre-Thatcher times. This is a disabling illusion, especially for the Left. The Thatcher project has certainly been exhausted, and the political energy by which it was animated in the early 1980s has evaporated, leaving only the dreary and unmeaning formulae of New Right ideology. Nevertheless Thatcherism has permanently changed the terms of political trade in Britain. It has ruled out any return either to traditional conservatism on the Right – One Nation Toryism, say – or to social democracy – a species of Croslandism or of Owenism, perhaps – on the Left. There can be no going back to Butskellism. Perhaps only a handful of observers, including a few perceptive Marxists, have grasped the paradoxical nature of Thatcherism. The project failed in almost all the main goals of its positive agenda. Yet, in conjunction with trends in the world economy which no government directs or controls, it transformed British society and public culture so as to render these earlier political projects, and even Thatcherism itself, anachronistic and redundant.

In many respects, Thatcherism was a self-undermining project. Those who formulated it did not perceive that the freeing of markets that drastically diminished the power of organised labour in Britain would have the unintended consequence, over time, of undermining economic security among the social groups who were Thatcherism's initial beneficiaries. It thereby worked to dissolve the electoral coalition of interests that had enabled it to come to power. The aspiring working class people who saw in Thatcherite policies the chance of upward social mobility into the middle classes, if they were successful in making the transition, discovered that the life of Middle England had been transformed beyond recognition. They emerged not in the sunlit uplands of bourgeois security, but onto a desolate plateau of middle class pauperdom. The poignant irony of Essex man and woman struggling up the economic escalator only to meet the bedraggled figures of the professional middle classes staggering down it is a narrative of our times that has yet to be fully chronicled. Thatcherism could not act as an instrument of social mobility for its initial supporters because it undid the class structure in terms of which they had framed their aspirations. That Thatcherism altered the British social landscape profoundly, unpredictably and irreversibly, is only a particularly dramatic illustration of the power of unfettered markets to unravel traditional forms of social life.

For all these reasons, those on the New Right who see political salvation – for themselves, if not for Britain – in reviving its lost verities are merely deluding themselves. The end of Thatcherism, which occurred, not suddenly with a bang when Thatcher herself was toppled in 1990, but slowly and with a whimper, during the long interregnum of the Major years, marked not only the political collapse of neoliberalism in Britain but also the closing of an era in its public culture. But to see that we must go beyond Thatcherism is also to see that there is no going back to social democracy.

It is a paradox of British political life that, at a moment in history when social democracy is in retreat everywhere, we are very nearly all social democrats now. In all parties, most of us have converged on a sensible and pragmatic middle ground, which in crucial respects already trails behind events. Social democracy was a political project whose stability and even identity depended on the geo-strategic environment of the Cold War. It defined its socialist content by its opposition both to Soviet communism and to American individualism. The Soviet collapse has removed this environment and denuded social democracy of the identity a bipolar world conferred on it. The new realities that spell ruin for the social-democratic project are the billions of industrious and skilled workers released onto the global market by the communist collapse and the disappearance of any effective barriers to the global mobility of capital. In this changed historical circumstance, the central economic programme of social democracy is unworkable and social democracy itself a bankrupt project.

It is true that the new social-democratic consensus in Britain represents a real advance on the sterile and atavistic debate between the Old Left and the New Right. Yet it is also a backward-looking perspective. In this essay I aim to clarify and explore the emerging social-democratic consensus in British public discourse. My purpose in so doing is not to endorse it. On the contrary it is to question it. Among the irreversible consequences of the Thatcherite project and its failure in Britain, one of the most neglected is the impossibility of any return to the policies and institutions of social democracy. In part, my argument is an historical one. Insofar as it was embodied in a labourist movement, social democracy is now a political project without an historical agent. The class base of social-democratic parties, not only in Britain but throughout Europe, has been eaten away by economic change. At the same time, the powers of national governments, which were the levers of social-democratic policy, have been steadily reduced. Though practising politicians inevitably find it hard to acknowledge it, the new global freedom of financial capital so hems in national governments as to limit severely, or to rule out altogether, traditional social-democratic full-employment policies. There is a dark historical irony in the fact of the formation of a social-democratic consensus at the very moment when both its class base and its political vehicle have been marginalised.

The risk of the emerging consensus is the hardening into a conventional wisdom of a set of assumptions which is as anachronistic as Thatcherism itself. The failure of neoliberal reforms of the welfare state either to diminish poverty or to control expenditure, both of which have risen inexorably, encourages the decent but misguided belief that the old British welfare state can be reinvented in another guise, and the hard choices of real welfare reform avoided. Neoliberal tolerance of long-term unemployment evokes the illusion that post-war full-employment policies can be revived and made effective. Crude neoliberal policies to reduce the size of the state failed in part because the impact of long-term unemployment on public expenditure was under-estimated. That failure obscures the unsustainability of a large and growing state in a period in which neither taxpayers nor lenders can be relied upon to finance public deficits. The absurdity and inhumanity of neoliberal policies to trim the size of government have produced a social-democratic complacency about its growth that is no less costly and dangerous.

The key test of whether we have yet formulated a genuinely post-Thatcherite political outlook is our ability to understand that, even as it undermined the conditions of its own political viability, Thatcherism at the same time destroyed other political projects (notably One Nation Toryism and social democracy) which had once been its rivals.

As yet, the shape of political life and public culture in Britain in the wake of the Thatcher project remains unclear. Nevertheless, several tendencies are already discernible. The fixed points of the social-democratic consensus, now accepted by the majority in all parties are:

● the unacceptable social costs and moral hazards of the unrestrained market individualism of the 1980s;
● the worldwide collapse of central-planning institutions, the economic vehicle of classical socialism;
● the universal rise – in a wide diversity of forms – of market institutions;
● and the acceptance that there is no possibility of returning to corporatist institutions and policies.

The failures of neo-corporatism in Britain, particularly in its tendency to generate distributional conflict rather than wealth creation, were the original political justification and historical rationale of Thatcherite policies. Within this cross-party social-democratic consensus, a movement of Tory modernisers currently seeks to apply a right-wing variant of the social-market philosophy to the tasks of legitimating the free market in political terms and extending market mechanisms further into the public sector. Among Labour's modernisers, a leading tendency seeks to modernise social democracy itself, by distinguishing between the policies and institutions in which it was embodied in the British post-war settlement and the central values of equality and community which remain constitutive of it as a political morality.

Beyond the social-democratic consensus, there is a group of right-wing radicals around John Redwood, no longer recognisably British Tories, who take their cue from American neoconservative cultural fundamentalists, aiming to renew New Right thought in another form. This second wave of New Right thinking rejects the sovereign individual of neoliberal ideology in favour of a return to 'traditional values', and seeks to buttress the institutions of the unfettered free market with restored forms of traditional family life. Whereas in the 1980s the New Right worked with the grain of the times, this revised form of New Right thought, while aiming to transcend the primitive market fundamentalism of neoliberal ideology, works against the culture of Britain in the 1990s. It sets itself against the dominant forces of the times in its denial of the pervasive demand for individual autonomy, in its revivalist response to the decay of inherited social forms, and its failure to understand that it is principally the subversive dynamism of market forces that is inexorably dissolving them. Within Labour, a dwindling band of classical socialists stands outside the social-democratic consensus, challenging the radical revisionism of the modernisers and rejecting social democracy as an unstable refinement of capitalism rather than a genuine alternative to it.

The modernising tendencies in both major parties need to run very fast simply to avoid being left far behind by events. The aim of this essay is to sketch a pattern of ideas whose chief merit may be that it is less removed from present circumstances than most. It advances a communitarian liberal perspective as one that avoids the principal errors of neoliberalism and enriches standard liberal philosophy with the distinctive insights of communitarian thinking. Its claim is that this perspective can aid thought on the central dilemma of the age: how can revolutionary changes in technology and the economy be reconciled with the enduring human needs for security and for forms of common life? Arising in a liberal culture, this dilemma can be expressed as that of balancing the interest in choice and autonomy, which are thought, often mistakenly, to be promoted by free markets, against the benefits, responsibilities and duties of community. The communitarian liberal view rejects both the economistic conception of the individual as a sovereign consumer and the legalist view of the individual as above all a rights-bearer. Recent American thought has combined these conceptions of the human subject within liberalism. The result may be a kind of liberalism, but not one that J.S. Mill or Alexis de Tocqueville, or Isaiah Berlin or Joseph Raz could recognise.

Communitarian liberalism departs from individualist liberalisms in that it conceives of choosing individuals as themselves creations of forms of common life. It rejects the libertarian view that individual choice must always be paramount over every other human need and interest. It is a misconception of market freedoms that they derive from the basic structure of human rights. It differs from conservative and neo-traditionalist communitarianisms[1] by acknowledging the strength and urgency of the need for individual autonomy. People voice and act upon that demand, to make their own choices and to be at least part authors of their own lives, in all of the institutions and practices of contemporary liberal societies. It recognises the pluralism of such cultures. Few of us are defined by membership of a single, all-embracing community, and there is no going back to any simpler, 'organic' way of life. It differs from social democracy by rejecting the egalitarian imposition of a single conception of justice in all contexts of economic and social life.

The key claim of communitarian liberalism is that the flourishing of individuals presupposes strong and deep forms of common life. The elements of the communitarian liberal perspective on which I shall focus are those that are especially salient to our present context. I consider and reject the neoliberal claim that markets necessarily enhance choice and autonomy. Instead I maintain that the liberal value of autonomy can be protected only in a public culture of which market exchange is but a subordinate part. To this extent, the conflict between autonomy and community is superficial. In the last section I shall consider areas of social life and public policy where this conflict is real and difficult. The central application of the communitarian liberal view to public policy is that market freedoms have instrumental value only, as a means to individual wellbeing. Moreover, they have this value only when they do not weaken forms of common life without which individual wellbeing is impoverished or impossible. Communitarian liberalism affirms that:

● individual autonomy presupposes a strong public culture in which choice and responsibility go together, and is realisable only as a common good;
● market exchange makes no inherent contribution to autonomy;
● therefore market competition must be limited in contexts, such as broadcasting and urban development, where its impact on individual autonomy may be disabling rather than enhancing;
● fairness demands the distribution of goods and responsibilities according to their common social meanings in particular contexts, thereby excluding market forces from domains (which might include the public provision of healthcare and education, for example) where they violate such common understandings.

These three claims express the distinctive communitarian political morality in which neither libertarian nor egalitarian principles are fundamental; rather the renewal and creation of worthwhile social forms is of the essence. The central insight of communitarian philosophy is that conceptions of autonomy and fairness are not embodiments of universal principles, but local understandings, grounded in particular forms of common life. Conceptions of autonomy and of fairness are local notions, both in the sense that they express the ethical life of specific cultures, and because their content varies greatly, depending on the domain of social activity in which they arise in any particular culture. In this morality, equality is demanded as a safeguard against exclusion. It is not, in social-democratic terms, a requirement of any theory of justice. The justice with which communitarian thinking is concerned is not universal. It is the local justice which matches goods to social understandings, as these arise in particular cultures and the specific domains of activity they contain. The autonomy which communitarian liberalism is concerned to protect and promote is not conceived, as it is in rights-based liberalism, as a claim in justice which has universal authority. Rather it is an element in individual wellbeing, as that has come to be understood and experienced in individualist cultures such as our own. It is a local virtue. By contrast with neoliberalism, the communitarian liberal view I advance here seeks to enrich autonomy and not merely to defend negative liberty. By contrast with social democracy, which has extended to social-welfare rights the supposedly unconditional claims of negative liberal rights, the communitarian view affirms the dependency of individual autonomy on a strong network of reciprocal obligations.

A fundamental implication of this communitarian liberal perspective is that market institutions are not freestanding but come embedded in the matrices of particular cultures and their histories. Market institutions will be politically legitimate only insofar as they respect and reflect the norms and traditions, including the sense of fairness, of the cultures whose needs they exist to serve. Legitimating the market requires that it be curbed or removed in institutions and areas of social life where common understandings demand that goods be distributed in accordance with ethical norms that the market necessarily disregards. Public acceptance of a dynamic market economy requires that the ethos of market exchange be excluded from important contexts. In those contexts non-market institutions and practices are to be protected as a matter of public policy.

These are propositions for whose general truth a

reasonable argument can be made out; but they are advanced here, not as elements in some impossible political *philosophia perennis*, but as topical antidotes to the chief dangers and errors of recent opinion and policy. They are meant to apply not universally but locally, in European liberal cultures, particularly that of Britain today.

The basic position of this essay is *pluralism*.[2] By this I do not mean the banal pluralism of interest groups celebrated in American democratic theory a generation ago. Instead I start from a pluralism which perceives and accepts conflicts among fundamental goods, diversity within and between cultures and traditions, and which sees this as a permanent condition to be lived with and enjoyed, not a prelude to some new kind of harmony. The overriding task we confront today is that of preserving, and extending, forms of common life, which highly individualist market institutions threaten to undermine or corrode. A connected task is that of developing common institutions in which different cultural traditions can coexist. In both of these cases, we will face unavoidable conflicts of values, uncombinable goods and choices among evils.

These conflicts of values compel revisions of the standard liberal, social-democratic and communitarian positions. The emerging British consensus, often shy of admitting radical conflict among fundamental values, is ill-prepared for such revisions. Any species of 'back-to-basics' communitarianism, which seeks a return to 'traditional values' or a restoration of vanished or dying forms of family or communal life, must be rejected as a form of nostalgia. Its fate in political life is likely to be no less farcical than that of the Tory 'back-to-basics' campaign. Any political project that aims to reinvent community in Britain today must be friendly (and the 'must' expresses here a requirement of political prudence as well as a dictate of morality) to sexual diversity, to the varieties of family life that the country harbours, and to its plurality of ethnic traditions and cultural forms.

19

Equally any form of social democracy which seeks across-the-board equality and denies the conflicts among equalities, such as that between achievable equality of opportunity and social mobility and unachievable educational equality which prohibits meritocratic selection in state schools, will be incoherent. In practice it will only sustain an unhealthy symbiosis of a semi-defunct class culture with soft-Left anti-elitism. Any liberal view which elevates the interest in individual autonomy above all others risks treating as inherently repressive communities and ways of life in which it is not so valued, such as those of some immigrant groups. In doing so it imposes a monoculturally liberal society rather than building pluralistic common institutions which are genuinely culturally diverse.

The task of the age is that of reconciling the human need for security with the permanent revolution of the market. This involves two other tasks: protecting common institutions whose ethos is not that of market exchange from the near-hegemony of market values in social life; and balancing the need for common life with the reality of deep cultural diversity.

The plurality of our cultural and ethical life means that we cannot recover (if we ever possessed) a common culture that is unified by any single world view or conception of the good. Nor can we, or should we, seek to reinstate any conception of national identity which expresses an earlier monocultural period of our history. We cannot recapture a 'thick' common culture grounded in a deep consensus on morality and history; but we must, if we are to avoid American social fragmentation, strengthen and develop a thinner, yet durable and resilient, common culture of shared understandings of fairness and tolerance. We cannot, and should not, hope to revive a 'traditional' form of family life that scarcely exists any longer, and which is in any case only one among the variety of kinds of families our society presently contains; but nor can we reasonably adopt the fashionable liberal ideal in which government is silent, or neutral, on the central issues of family life. A pluralist state can have few core ethical commitments; but a commitment to the family – in all its legitimate diversity – must be one of them. Government must have, and act upon, a view of the 'thin' culture of obligations and responsibilities that family life in all its forms presupposes, even as it acts to nurture diversity in the kinds of family. Only if it does this can a pluralist state be one in which different forms of common life coexist peacefully in shared common institutions and have a decent chance of renewing itself across the generations.

Reconciling diversity with commonality will require institution-building as well as institution-repair, along with creativity and imagination in the making of public policy. The theorist's task is to engage in preparatory thinking which might assist those who share their political objectives. It is not to develop policy. At the same time, the historical and theoretical perspective outlined here does have some broad implications for policy. Of these, three are worth signposting.

Firstly, the claim that fairness is local and contextual and has to do with distributing goods according to their common social meanings has clear implications on policy in health care. It leads us clearly to condemn the commercialisation of the National Health Service. In education it supports the argument that forms of meritocratic selection can and should be reintroduced in state schools.

Secondly, it is central to this perspective that market institutions unavoidably and desirably reflect and express particular cultures and their histories. This argues against many social-democratic proposals for the wholesale grafting onto British economic life of practices which have been successful in other cultural and political contexts, such as those of Germany and Japan, and against the federalist project for European institutions. In the post-socialist age, the choices we face are not between central planning and the market economy but between varieties of capitalism. Yet we do not have the freedom to combine as we choose the distinct virtues of capitalisms which express different cultures and their histories. In Britain our task must be to make the liberal market capitalism, our historic inheritance, friendlier to human needs.

Thirdly, although the traditional social-democratic commitment to full employment cannot now be implemented, the goal of achieving a fair distribution of work (which is now one of the most important goods of all in our society) and a benefits system that is seen to be just in that it incorporates notions of reciprocity, is now paramount. In each of these three areas, the goal is to protect in new ways human interests once served by social democracy, and to do so without allowing the task of mediating conflicts among these interests to be distorted by the classical social-democratic commitment to overall equality.

The sphere of life in which these unavoidable conflicts are negotiated and resolved is that of politics. There is a standard Anglo-American liberal philosophy that conflicts between rival human interests and between divergent conceptions of the good and their associated forms of common life can be arbitrated by appeal to a theory of justice or rights. This idea is expressed in contemporary social-democratic demands for a constitutional revolution in Britain.[3] In the communitarian liberal view I advance, constitutional reform is desirable and even indispensable, insofar as it protects fundamental freedoms by incorporating the European Convention into British law, makes accountable the 'new magistracy' of the quango state and devolves power to Scotland and Wales.

These important reforms can be achieved, however, through existing institutions of parliamentary government in an unfixed constitution, as aspects of the new political settlement Britain needs. Of course, national government is not the only, nor always the most important, domain of political life. It is imperative that political initiative be devolved to lower levels of government and to non-governmental institutions. But the purpose is to devolve power and enhance accountability. It would be wrong to use these reforms to remove issues of public policy from political life and transfer them to the jurisdiction of the courts, as has been tried, with predictably ruinous consequences, in the American culture of legalism.

The most important measure in a new political settlement is not constitutional but electoral reform. In the pluralist and communitarian view defended here, a major weakness of social-democratic thought is the 'constitutionalist illusion'. This is the idea that legal institutions can remove the necessity for recurrent political renegotiation to balance competing interests. After all necessary constitutional reforms, the real task is the political one of searching for the elusive thread of common life through the labyrinth of intractably conflicting interests and ideals.

What social democracy was

Social democracy was a complex structure of ideas, policies, institutions and objectives embodied in the social and political settlements in a number of west-European countries during the post-war period up to the end of the 1980s. Its intellectual roots were in late nineteenth- and early twentieth-century revisions of classical Marxism and socialism. The most important of these were the rejection, on grounds both of practicability and of its incompatibility with democracy, of nationalisation and central planning of the economy. Social democracy recognised a century ago that classical socialism was dead. Today we are witnessing the crisis and decomposition of social democracy, the successor to classical socialism. In particular, the social-democratic character of European institutions, in which many British social democrats have invested most of their political hopes, has in the past decade and a half been compromised almost to vanishing point. The European Union has increasingly come to adopt neoliberal ideology, and distinctively social-democratic policies have suffered irreversible setbacks in several European countries, including France and Sweden. What then was social democracy? How and why has it ended ?

Its central objectives and policies were these:

- the pursuit of greater equality of income and wealth through redistributive tax and welfare policies;
- the promotion of full employment through economic growth;
- a 'cradle-to-grave' welfare state defended as the social embodiment of citizen rights;
- and support for and cooperation with a strong labour movement as the principal protector of workers' interests.

In the post-war period up to the early 1970s, social democracy appropriated Keynesian thought to provide it with a coherent and viable economic programme, the lack of which during the interwar period had condemned it to paralysis in the face of the Great Depression and rout when confronted by fascism and National Socialism. In Britain, the decay of social democracy came perhaps to a considerable extent from within. There the triangular collusion of employers, unions and government in corporatism generated not industrial cooperation and wealth creation, as it did in post-war Germany and Austria, but conflict and decline. However, the constraints of the world market supplemented these internal failings, and brought the British corporatist experiment to a close, when in 1976 the IMF was called in. These external constraints rule out not only any return to corporatism in Britain but also any reversion to the classic economic policies of social democracy.

The social-democratic economic programme – most centrally, promoting full employment by stimulating investment through a policy of deficit financing – has ceased to be sustainable. The aborted Mitterand expansion in the early 1980s, and the comprehensive collapse of the Swedish model in the early 1990s, suggest that the power of the international currency and bond markets is now sufficient to interdict any such expansionist policies. In economic theory this is hardly news. It was recognised by both Kalecki and Keynes that the international mobility of financial capital undercuts full-employment policy. Yet the practical implications of the power of world markets to constrain national policies are more urgent now than ever. It is no exaggeration to say that the global freedom of capital effectively demolishes the economic foundations of social democracy.

The underlying political morality of social democracy was eclectic in its origins and contents, and differed in its emphases from country to country and from time to time. For example, the relations with trade unions were unique in Germany, partly because the institutional slate was wiped clean after the Nazi period. Yet in general the social democratic ideal was a form of society-wide egalitarian community of which the workplace community was conceived to be the germ. Without this animating egalitarian political morality, social democracy is nothing. Although many social-democratic parties in government were content merely to contain or moderate the economic inequalities thrown up by market capitalism, their ideal remained that of compressing income and wealth inequalities.

They did not make much progress toward this egalitarian objective, any more than they were successful in eradicating poverty, though matters would arguably have been even worse in the absence of social-democratic policies. In other areas, such as housing clearance programmes that shattered working class street communities and education policies which prohibited meritocratic selection, social-democratic policies probably worked against the values they were meant to serve. It can be argued that social-democratic welfare institutions, like later neoliberal policies, have had the effect of institutionalising poverty rather than removing its causes. Many social-democratic policies to promote equality have proved either futile or counterproductive. Not only the historic policies but also the constitutive morality of social democracy have been rendered utopian by the ruling forces of the age.

Social democrats and neoliberals share the weakness

that they are unwilling to admit the reality of conflicts between central goods and values insofar as they limit the options for public policy. That the promotion of a more mobile, less stratified and so more equal society might conflict with egalitarian policies in state schools is a discomforting proposition few social democrats are willing to entertain. It implies what is manifestly true, but also uncomfortable: that equality is not of a piece but complex; worse, that one equality, one demand of justice, may compete with another.

Britain's position as an ill-equipped and deskilled country in a desperately competitive world market would make the political projects of a less straitened past hopeless and unworkable, even if Thatcherism had not already seen them off. It is this reality and the recognition by the politically decisive voters in Middle England, that present and past policies are leading them to not-so-genteel poverty, that rule out a reversion to the policies of the post-war settlement, just as much as the constraints of global bond and currency markets. Keynesian deficit financing is interdicted by the bond markets and any attempt to shore up the Beveridge settlement will be undone by voter resistance to increased taxation. Higher public expenditure in certain welfare state institutions, such as the NHS, is highly desirable, but it will be politically sustainable only if reforms in other areas allow it to be incurred without a substantially higher tax burden. These are dilemmas with which the social-democratic policies of a decade or a generation ago cannot help us.

For these reasons, it is unlikely a future Labour government's policies would resemble the One Nation Toryism of a generation ago, or those of British Social Democrats in the 1980s. These are obsolete positions, no more available to Labour than primitive neoliberalism is now to the Conservatives. Labour is more likely to try to fuse the individualist economic culture of liberal capitalism with communitarian concerns about fairness and community. But can such a combination be made stable? Just such a fusion was envisaged in the 'New Liberalism' of J.A. Hobson and L.T. Hobhouse at the beginning of this century. The goal of the New Liberalism was to harness the wealth-creating dynamism of liberal capitalism while using the powers of the sovereign state to constrain it and temper its impact on social cohesion. It was this New Liberal vision, developed in the interwar period in the Liberal Summer Schools, which informed the Beveridge-Keynes settlement that emerged from the Second World War and endured for a generation into the mid-1970s. At the century's end, the global mobility of capital, and its power to constrain the freedom of action of sovereign states in economic policy, is vastly greater. Keynesian macroeconomic policies and the Beveridgean welfare state are pillars of a *status quo ante* that has been destroyed irrecoverably. Can something akin to the New Liberal vision be re-embodied in the *fin de siecle* context of swiftly advancing globalisation?

Right, left and globalisation

One of the starting-points of my inquiry is a contradiction within neoliberal policy over the past decade and a half. The neoliberal contradiction arises from trying to support both deregulated markets on the one hand and inherited cultural traditions, allegiances and hierarchical forms of social order on the other.

Though not predictable in detail, the impact of deregulated markets, in labour for example, is to alter the relative rewards of different social groups, and thereby to disappoint established expectations. This is one example of the ways in which the free market subverts inherited class hierarchies and deferences. Of course, technological innovation, and planning decisions in a command economy, will have similar effects. The point is that in present circumstances deregulated market institutions make changes in relative rewards a rapid and continuous process that makes a culture of deference, of the sort embodied in the British class system, dysfunctional and in the long run, unsustainable.

The marketisation of intermediary institutions and professions which have hitherto regulated themselves more by ethos and trust than upon contract has had an analogous impact. Though the tension between freeing markets and preserving or renewing a tradition-bound social order arises naturally within nation-states, it is more severe in its effects when public policy acts to open domestic economies to global markets.

The neoliberal contradiction is greater in a context of globalisation partly because it yields incoherent conceptions of the state. William Rees-Mogg states the view of the New Right with refreshing candour, when he observes: 'The twentieth century nation-state, taking and often wasting half the citizens' money, is a dying social form.'[4] He does not pause to ask what will replace this dying social form as a focus of citizens' allegiance. In this he is typical of neoliberal thinking.[5] In this strain of thought, the sovereign nation-state exists to express and support national culture, yet it accepts no responsibility for the renewal of cultural traditions, for the protection of citizens from economic risk (apart perhaps from the provision of a subsistence income), or for the survival of distinctive communities and forms of livelihood. (The Swiss interest in preserving small-scale and economically inefficient forms of agriculture as an important motive for their remaining outside the EU, can find no expression in neoliberal policy. If the free global market so dictates, such livelihoods must go to the wall, along with the communities they support.)

The neoliberal state is minimalist and non-interventionist in economic policy, confining itself ideally to the custody of the rules defining and promoting market competition. But, at the same time, its social policy may penalise one-parent families, and tight immigration controls may bolster those traditional institutions and forms of culture on which market institutions themselves may in the past have depended for their effective functioning and popular legitimacy.

New Right ideology neglects the many ways in which market freedoms have required, in Britain and elsewhere, the centralisation of power and initiative in strong, often authoritarian, state institutions. It is not accidental that local government in Britain has almost been destroyed, that many intermediary institutions have been denuded of much of their autonomy and distinctive ethos by the creation of internal quasi-markets, or that the Quango State has emerged. These are integral components of neoliberalism. After all, neoliberalism was the political expression of the belief that market exchange is the primordial form of human freedom. Political freedom and freedom of voice in autonomous institutions were suspect freedoms, compared with the freedoms of exchange, and it was wholly legitimate to curb them when market exchange could thereby be extended. It was by this primitive logic that there arose the familiar paradox of market libertarianism, in which it generated a species of authoritarian individualism resting on the political foundation of a centralist state. Macaulay's observation that the gallows and the hangman stand at the back of James Mill's utilitarian state seems premonitory of the neoliberal minimum state, in which the privatised prison and the Next Steps Agency's accountants fulfil similar functions.

In its applications to intermediary institutions, neoliberal policy from Thatcher to Major has been one of neo-nationalisation. Autonomous institutions of all kinds have been subjected to centralised direction by the imposition on them of a regime of quasi-markets. This regime of market corporatism is the ironic upshot of a project whose original impulse came from a revulsion against the failing corporatism of the 1970s. Future historians are likely to be impressed by the speed with which the market Bolshevism of the early 1980s generated the Tory managerial nomenklatura of the early 1990s. No less ironic is the way a Tory defence of national sovereignty was yoked to a policy of opening up the economy to the full rigours of globalisation. Deeper integration into the EU was opposed because it was believed (falsely, on current evidence) that the EU might be protectionist, and would thereby inhibit globalisation in Britain. In this neoliberal view, national sovereignty must be defended from the encroachments of European institutions, in order that it might more comprehensively be abandoned through a complete surrender to global market forces. These sorry posturings illustrate the core neoliberal contradiction between economic globalisation and national sovereignty.

The social-democratic contradiction mirrors the neoliberal one. Economic globalisation removes, or weakens, the policy levers whereby social-democratic governments sought to bring about social solidarity and egalitarian redistribution. Full employment cannot be promoted by aggressive deficit financing because that is now being interdicted by global bond markets (as the Swedish social democrats discovered). Using the tax system to promote goals of income and wealth redistribution is severely constrained by unprecedented international mobility of capital and people. Globalisation weakens or undermines the bargaining power of organised labour. Public financing of the welfare state is constrained by dependency on global capital markets, which limit to a narrow range national governments' leverage over interest rates and exchange rates. The magnitudes of these effects of globalisation on national economies and governments remain controversial. What is less controversial is the conviction that they will become ever more significant in future.

There is an insoluble contradiction within contemporary social democracy between economic globalisation and egalitarian community. It is hyperbolic to claim, as many do, that sovereign states lack any leverage on national economic life. Nevertheless it remains plausible that the inheritance of neoliberal deregulation, together with ongoing globalisation, constrain or remove many of the policy levers on which social-democratic governments have hitherto relied. More particularly, they make the distributional goals of social democracy unachievable, at least by traditional social-democratic means. Furthermore, the impact on the labour market of neoliberal deregulation and (though this is as yet probably small) of globalisation make the workplace-based conception of community that was traditionally defended by social democrats less practically sustainable, and less centrally relevant than before.

Globalisation undermines both the Left project of egalitarian community and the Right project of reproducing authoritative institutions in a social context of market-generated economic inequalities. This is so, however globalisation is conceived or measured – by the magnitude of flows of trade, capital or migration, or as a massive extension of processes of marketisation of social life that have long been in evidence within national economic cultures. It may be that meeting the human need for enduring forms of common life will ultimately require the imposition of political limits on aspects of globalisation, such as global free trade. The present consensus will at once reject these as both unworkable and dangerously illiberal. However that may be, globalisation poses undeniably fundamental challenges, encompassing novel possibilities both of human servitude and of emancipation, for which contemporary political thought on all parts of the spectrum is very ill prepared.

The diversity of market institutions

Now that the rivalry between the market economy and central planning has been decisively settled, there is a common perception that systemic competition now goes on between different forms of market institutions, or between capitalisms. There is no single, ideal type of market institution to which all market economies are evolving, but rather a diversity of market institutions. Each has its own distinctive achievements and hazards, but all are engaged in a global competition. As far as it goes, this perception is well founded. It rightly rejects the view that there is any model of market institutions, that of American individualist market capitalism, say, to which the whole world is inexorably moving. In the end there is no such thing as the free market, but rather a variety of cultural institutions and legal devices and instruments through which economic life is mediated. This is indeed the core of the theoretical insights preserved by the 'social market' tradition, for which I have myself in the past argued.[6] The key proposition of social market theory, that 'the market' is not a freestanding institution, the expression of unrestricted human freedom and rationality in the economic realm, but instead an abstraction from an enormous miscellany of practices and institutions having deep roots in social life, remains valid and important.

The social market perspective expands our awareness of the range of possibilities for market institutions and their associated economic cultures. It becomes misleading when it is deployed to support policies and reforms aiming to make eclectic borrowings from other market institutions, with a view to enhancing the performance of those we inherit. The social market perspective ought to work as a theoretical constraint on such eclecticism, because it insists upon the embeddedness of market institutions in cultural traditions over which public policy has little leverage. Paradoxically, social democrats who disregard this constraint imposed on policy are at one with neoliberals in their neglect of the cultural matrices of economic life. They share with neoliberals a rationalistic and utopian project of harmonising market institutions according to the requirements of an ideal model.

These social-democratic conceptions are expressed in their project for European institutions, which is to extend the Rhine model of capitalism across the European Union, regardless of national cultural differences. This project rests on the illusion that there exists presently in continental Europe a viable and functioning model of market institutions that is a feasible alternative to the deformed individualist institutions which we inherited from the Thatcher era. Underlying this, there is the deeper illusion that market institutions are neutral pieces of institutional machinery which can be moved freely around the world and adopted eclectically as elements in public policy. This is a mirage. Market institutions, like political ones, are not detachable from their histories and parent cultures. They are deeply embedded in them, and remain always integral expressions of them. The ruling error of the Thatcher project was the supposition that American market institutions could be transplanted to Britain. Yet Britain's vastly different history, its lack of the American culture of mobility, geographical and occupational, and its distinctively European conception of the role of government in civil society precluded this. It is imperative that this error of the New Right should not be replicated on the Left, in an analogously misconceived and foredoomed attempt to transplant to Britain the market institutions of Germany or Japan.

There no longer exists a 'European model' which could be replicated in Britain. In continental Europe the social-democratic and social-market traditions are in long-term retreat and have not solved central problems which we share with other European countries such as mass structural unemployment. There can surely be no more vivid example of this retreat than contemporary Sweden. There, both the active labour policy and the collective wage bargaining policies central to social democracy in that country have suffered such a complete collapse that there is now nothing to which the expression 'Swedish model' could any longer refer. As a consequence, economic life in Sweden is now evolving ineluctably towards the neoliberal norm increasingly dominant in the rest of Europe, with all its costs and hazards.

Recent strategic and geopolitical developments are crucial in accounting for the mounting problems of European institutions. Both European social democracy and Christian democracy belong to an epoch – the Cold War period – that is now a fading memory. Indeed, the difficulties European 'social market' economies, including Germany, are having in adapting to global competition are themselves direct consequences of the end of the Cold War, as billions of producers previously shut off from the world economy have now entered it as full participants. European social democracy probably required for its survival an historical niche – the strategic environment of the Cold War – which has now vanished. The intense pressure to adopt neoliberal policies in all European Union countries may be explicable in part by the new intensity of the competition which those countries face from low-wage but often high-skilled post-communist countries. It is this altered geopolitical environment, more than any other single factor, that explains the neoliberal evolution of European policy and institutions. For it greatly reinforces the changes in social structure, and particularly in the relative position of industrial labour, that in Continental Europe as much as in Britain have all but destroyed the old class base of social democracy. For all these interrelated reasons, it is a serious mistake for social democrats who despair of neoliberal hegemony in public policy in Britain to look to European institutions as a *deus ex machina*.

Moreover, German and Japanese-type market institutions are themselves evolving. There is now no stable German or Japanese model that could be exported. This is not to say that the Rhine model of capitalism, say, is in terminal decline, or is bent on convergence with Anglo-Saxon economic culture. Such prognoses, common as they are among neoliberals, are extremely implausible. The German achievement in absorbing the GDR rustbelt, despite the policy mistakes which accompanied it, is almost certainly beyond the reach of any other economy in the world (aside perhaps from that of Japan). It certainly does not suggest a system in inexorable decline. However, the current problems of the German economy suggest clearly, as David Goodhart observes in his sympathetic examination of the Rhine model, that 'the future of the social market is certainly not guaranteed'.[7] If or when the Rhine model renews itself in a novel form, it will be able to do so by virtue of cultural traditions of consensual/managerial politics that cannot be reproduced in Britain. The Rhine model is sustained by these solidaristic cultural traditions, because it embodies a balance among interests which becomes unstable if any one of them is excluded. The likelihood must be faced that the Rhine model is an historical singularity, owing much to the institutional void arising after the destruction of the Nazi regime. For that and many other reasons, it cannot be replicated anywhere else in Europe.

For different reasons, Japanese market institutions are no less of a singularity. The social contract in contemporary Japan, far from being immemorial, emerged from the intense industrial and political conflicts of the immediate post-war period. It has succeeded in keeping unemployment levels uniquely low by subsidising employment practices that are 'economically inefficient'. It is highly probable, and no less desirable, that Japan will resist the importation of Western, and more particularly American, employment policies, even if the current forms of lifelong job-holding must of necessity be modified. But the Japanese strategy of reconciling the labour mobility produced by technological innovation and international competition with job security for the majority of the population is not open to us. It depends, among other things, on cultural traditions, in family life and the relations of individuals with communities, that we cannot emulate. The most successful aspects of German and Japanese economic policy seem in fact to be those which are least exportable.[8]

The project of adapting and reforming our individualist market institutions to meet these enduring human needs is inhibited by the social-democratic belief that there is, or may yet be, a single European model of market institutions, to which Britain could assimilate. French and German capitalism are not subtypes of a single European model with which Anglo-Saxon capitalism can be usefully contrasted. In what respects are the economic cultures of Sweden and Austria, say, similar to those of Greece and Portugal? The objective of 'harmonising' these market institutions is a rationalist utopia, since it involves ironing out cultural differences of which diversity in market institutions is a natural expression.

Of course, European capitalisms possess common features distinguishing them from American and East-Asian capitalisms and from the anarcho-capitalisms that have emerged in post-communist Russia and China. The manifest foundering of the European federalist project should enable us to see that the future for distinctively European capitalism is in a diversity of market institutions and not in a single uniform pattern. The project of constructing federal institutions in Europe, particularly a single European currency, will probably come to shipwreck on conflicts of national interest, most crucially between France and Germany. The wave of public sector strikes in France in December 1995, though it has not yet produced a change of direction within the French political elite, has shown how costly, in social as well as economic terms, the Franco-German axis has already proven for France. Once they are reflected in voting behaviour, it is more than likely that these costs will delay, or even perhaps derail, the project of a single currency. The reality is that the social costs of that project are such that it cannot in the end be politically legitimated even in the countries that are its core supporters. As yet, however, a post-federalist project for Europe which recognises these realities has hardly begun to be formulated.[9]

In the longer term, the Gaullist idea of a *Europe des patries* may come to be as obsolete as European federalism is today, and there may be a Europe of regions within a confederal framework. But for the foreseeable future, the rock on which the European federalist project will run aground is the reality of Europe's sovereign nation-states, and their conflicting interests. However enfeebled national political cultures and institutions have become in recent years, they remain the central forum of democratic political participation. There is no transnational European political culture, and therefore attempts to plug the 'democratic deficit' in European institutions will come to nothing. The only likely future for Europe is one of sometimes unstable sovereign states having both common and conflicting interests, whose relations with one another will be governed by the classical logic of the balance of power.

Manifestly, a new European project would entail abandonment of the core project of European federalism, the proposal for a single (as opposed to a common) European currency. From the communitarian standpoint advanced here, the chief argument against such a single currency is that it would be deflationary and would lead to areas of high unemployment. It would be tolerable and workable only if it was combined with an EU-wide labour market with genuine mass labour mobility. Such continental labour mobility will be rejected by most Europeans, both electorally and in their own behaviour, because of its social costs and disruptive consequences for local communities and personal attachments. The social-democratic project of a single European currency shares with neoliberal policies a rationalistic disdain for such attachments and communities. Its practical results would be indistinguishable from those associated in Britain with Thatcherite policies. This is perceived by the Right everywhere in Europe apart from Britain. In Sweden, as in other European countries, the Right supports the development of transnational European institutions because they rightly believe that they will embody neoliberal policies. Opposition to them is confined largely to left-wing communitarian nationalists. It is a comment on the parochialism of British political life that social democrats have accepted the Thatcherite claim that opposition to European federalism is the prerogative of the Right.

The social-democratic project of extending the Rhine model of capitalism across the European Union is as utopian as the neoliberal one of harmonising European economies on an agenda of deregulation and competition. Both evade the reality of diverse national economic cultures in Europe. Both suppress the huge costs, large risks and certain failure of any project of remodelling the varieties of market institutions which Europe contains on any single pattern. The idea that the nations and regions of the European Union can come together in a single economic culture is, in fact, as remote from any historic reality or likelihood as the notion that its institutions contain the makings of a single political culture. Public policy which neglects the cultural dimensions of market institutions will also fail to perceive and realise genuine possibilities of reforming them so that they are more friendly to human needs.

Welfare, local justice and complex fairness

The variety of market institutions is denied or trivialised in neoliberal ideology, which shares a commitment to economic reductionism with vulgar Marxism. Tacitly or expressly, neoliberal thought anticipates and welcomes global convergence on individualist market capitalism on a single pattern – typically the American model. It is able to adopt this simplistic position because of its economistic understanding of the relations between market institutions and cultural life. Social life everywhere is understood according to a model of market exchange.

This is itself an illicit generalisation from one historic variety of market economy, roughly that of England during the last few centuries, and of countries to which English market institutions were successfully exported. It fails to recognise that flourishing market institutions might be accompanied by, or even depend upon, non-individualist forms of social and moral life. It was unable to anticipate that freeing markets would fracture communities, deplete ethos and trust within institutions, and finally mute or thwart the economic renewal which free markets were supposed to generate.

Neoliberal welfare policy actually reinforced these forces by submitting welfare to the abstract calculus of market exchange.

New Right thought about welfare contained three cardinal misconceptions. It imagined that the human interest in rising income and increased consumer choice, which the free market supposedly protects and promotes, always outweighs that in controlling economic risk. It understood welfare institutions as mechanisms for income-transfer or poverty relief, rather than as devices for security against common risks and the dangers of exclusion. Accordingly it favoured selectivity in welfare provision that carried with it huge incentive costs and the moral hazard of creating cultures of dependency where none had existed before. Rejecting the very idea of social justice as alien to market freedoms, and indifferent or complacent about the impact of these freedoms on social cohesion, it neglected the vital role of welfare institutions in counteracting the indifference of unfettered market exchange to fairness, and so promoting social solidarity and common citizenship.

All three errors arose from a common cause. This is the neoliberal *canard* that markets are freestanding social relationships, embodying individual freedom and the human propensity to trade to mutual advantage. This fundamental error of neoliberal thought accounts for the inability of neoliberal policy to perceive that markets generate systemic economic risks and a pervasive sense of unfairness even when they produce rising incomes. A dynamic market economy can be politically legitimated, in a democratic regime such as that of contemporary Britain, only insofar as it is complemented by institutions and policies which counteract these hazards, and which remove market competition from some social contexts altogether.

Policies based on these neoliberal errors have been highly counterproductive even in their own terms. In New Zealand, policies based on the conception of welfare institutions as mere income transfer mechanisms, in conjunction with other neoliberal measures, have managed to create a dependent underclass where none had hitherto existed. This was the result of a feature of all means-tested welfare institutions. They create poverty traps in which perverse incentives imprison welfare recipients in dependency. Universal welfare institutions, of which the National Health Service prior to the Conservatives' neoliberal reforms is perhaps the best example, carry no such hazards with them. (Nor do they carry the large administrative costs of targeted systems.) Because neoliberal thought conceives of welfare institutions solely as devices for poverty relief, it cannot avoid remodelling them in ways that institutionalise poverty itself.

These counterproductive results are not accidental. They arise from the libertarian political morality of neo-liberals, in which any state expenditure other than that on narrowly public goods is inherently suspect. Welfare expenditures are particularly suspect because of their allegedly perverse distributional effects, when benefits are extended to those who are not yet poor. The benefits of well-conceived universal schemes in promoting social integration and preventing poverty are not perceived, even when (as with the NHS) such universal schemes are far more cost-effective and less wasteful than targeted schemes in other countries. Neoliberal policy shares with egalitarian social democracy a fixation on such distributional issues. This distributional preoccupation effectively occludes the vital role of welfare institutions in cementing social solidarity in an age in which all forms of common life are challenged by individualism.

Hayekian theory was able to deny the necessity, even the meaningfulness, of social justice, in part because it imagined that the sheer productivity of unfettered markets would preclude any crisis of legitimacy of capitalist institutions. It treated deep-seated and long-standing popular sentiments of fairness, of the sort that were expressed in revulsion against the poll tax, as unfortunate atavisms, which if they do not die out are best stamped out. Like egalitarianism, it conceived social justice in comprehensive and monistic terms, dictating patterns of distribution across the whole of social life and activity. Social democrats have a similar conception, understanding social justice in terms of approximation to some across-the-board principle of equality.[10]

Both neoliberalism and social democracy understand fairness in simple and global terms, as embodied in libertarian rights or else in a principle of equality. I have argued elsewhere that neither libertarian nor egalitarian principles can be fundamental in a credible political morality.[11] The contents of rights depend on claims about the relative urgency of competing human interests which are inherently controversial. Conceptions of negative rights to liberty, and of a minimum state which protects such rights, are irredeemably indeterminate. Egalitarian principles are no less indeterminate, concealing conflicts among important equalities. Moreover egalitarian principles implausibly attach moral importance to purely relational properties, when what has moral importance is wellbeing. If satiable human needs can be met, no global, overarching principle of distribution is necessary or plausible.[12] This does not mean that distributional principles can be altogether dispensed with. It means that, where issues of distribution unavoidably arise, norms of fairness figure as shared understandings of the meanings of social goods, as these arise in specific domains of activity in particular cultural contexts.

In addition to such philosophical arguments, the central historical thesis argued here is that global freedom of capital, and to an increasing degree, of labour, restricts radically the leverage of sovereign states in pursuing social-democratic egalitarian goals.[13] Yet any government concerned with stability and cohesion in social life is bound to have regard to the levels of economic inequality produced by its policies. Some part of the phenomenal growth in economic inequality in the 1980s was avoidable. (It is noteworthy that the only comparable country which suffered a larger increase in economic inequality than Britain in the 1980s was New Zealand, in which neoliberal policies were even more relentlessly and consistently pursued.) No less significant is the role played by the popular perception of vastly increased levels of economic inequality in Russia in explaining the results of Russia's parliamentary elections in December 1995, in which the parties sponsoring liberal market reform policies were humililiated. Concern with levels of economic inequality is dictated by concern for common life; but it does not mandate a strategy of equalisation; a strategy which the diminished leverage of sovereign states makes probably unworkable anyway.

The unattainability of social-democratic ideals of equality does not imply that a stable society can do without norms of fairness. On the contrary, such norms are essential. But they must be local and contextual, not universal or global, and reflect shared social understandings.[14] Such shared local understandings are by no means always conservative in their implications for policy. Consider here two salient examples.

In Britain most people think it unfair that access to decent medical care should be restricted by income rather than need, or the provision of such care should be distorted by market forces. This common understanding condemns the neoliberal commercialisation of the NHS, if – as available evidence strongly suggests – the introduction of market mechanisms within it has partly decoupled patient care from medical need and made access to care to a significant degree an accident of the policies of the NHS Trust currently in force in one's locality. Moreover, it demands the reversal of these policies, insofar as they have effects which violate it. (I do not mean to suggest that there is a NHS status quo to which we can return. None such can be recovered in health policy, any more than it can in any other area of policy. A reintegrated NHS would inevitably be very different from that which neoliberal policy destroyed.) This understanding does not condemn the very existence of private medicine; but it does condemn policies which result in access to decent medical care depending on factors other than need, such as patients' income.

Consider secondly the social understanding in Britain that the appropriate criteria for allocating educational opportunity are meritocratic. We do not auction places at university and the American practice of imposing ethnic quotas on university admissions is not on any policy agenda. Moreover, this understanding of fairness in education condemns policies which make access to good schooling contingent on income.

Yet our class inequalities are reproduced through a large private sector in schooling, and reinforced by an egalitarian prohibition on meritocratic policies in state schools. Where strict limits are imposed on the pursuit of egalitarian goals through the tax system, and widening income inequality allows an increasing percentage of the middle classes to opt out of the state system, there is an irresolvable conflict between educational egalitarianism and the pursuit of a broader social equality. (I am taking for granted that the freedom to found and patronise private schools cannot be infringed upon. It is in any case a freedom protected by international treaties to which Britain is a signatory.) This is a real conflict of equalities that social democrats are very shy of admitting. If the prospects of egalitarian redistribution through the tax system are now severely limited, growing economic and social inequality can be averted only by an improvement in the primary skills of the most disadvantaged and excluded groups.

It is impossible to accept, as many social democrats claim, that a greater commitment of resources to state schools can by itself achieve this objective. The practical result of social-democratic opposition to meritocratic policies in state schools can then only be the development of an increasingly stratified society, in which educational privilege and educational egalitarianism coexist in an unhealthy symbiosis. Such an outcome, in which British class culture is perpetuated by the anti-elitism of the soft Left, must be a defeat for the social-democratic ideal of equal opportunity.[15] The reintroduction of meritocratic policies in state schools can therefore be defended in social-democratic egalitarian terms as a vital aid to equal opportunity. It can be defended also in communitarian terms, as it would diminish the incentives to opt out, and thereby increase the inclusiveness of state schooling. By promoting participation in common institutions, the adoption of meritocratic policies in state schools could further social mobility without sacrificing social cohesion. It could achieve these results, fundamentally because it accords with the sense of fairness regarding educational opportunity which informs the common culture.

I do not argue that appealing to shared understandings of fairness in particular social domains or contexts resolves all questions of social justice. Quite the opposite: the claims of local justice may be conflicting. My argument for complex fairness is that there are hard choices arising from these conflicts, and that there is no overarching theory or principle by which such conflicts can be arbitrated.

Within healthcare, choices must be made about the relative urgency of different medical needs. Common understandings of what is fair cannot help us much there. An unintended beneficial consequence of neoliberal reform of the NHS is that it has made transparent the rationing and prioritisation that have always existed but have gone unscrutinised and undebated. These hard choices are not greatly assisted by appeal to shared understandings, partly because the development of medical technologies has run far ahead of public awareness and there is nothing akin to moral common sense in regard to many of the possibilities they have opened up.

There is another reason why shared contextual understandings cannot resolve all important issues about fairness. In a culture as deeply pluralistic as ours, there are contexts in which no common understanding exists, or in which the inherited understanding is strongly contested. Familial and sexual contexts are the most obvious of these. Others concerned with the value of human life, or the relations of human beings with other animal species, may be no less important. Many of these hard choices are undecidable by any theory of justice or rights because they are conceived differently by people with different world views and conceptions of the good.

Religious believers who attach intrinsic and unique worth to human life will understand conflicts of medical priorities involving life-saving differently from those who attach no such moral importance to it. Finally, even where there is cultural consensus on the domains within which goods are properly allocated, they may make conflicting demands on scarce resources which can be resolved only by a collective political decision. In those circumstances, a public conversation is needed, with the aim of generating a sense of fairness that can be shared even by people with very different substantive moral outlooks.

We have no alternative to engaging in ongoing public discourse, in which a provisional settlement is reached, and recurrently renegotiated, on such issues. Forms of liberal thought which imagine that such issues can be resolved by the development of a 'theory of justice', or a 'theory of rights', are trading in illusions. Such liberalisms foster a legalist and constitutionalist mirage, in which the delusive certainty of legal principles is preferred to the contingencies and compromises of political practice, where a settlement among communities and ways of life, always temporary, can alone be found. This primacy of the political sphere in the communitarian conception is an insuperable objection to all standard forms of liberal thought, including the Rawlsian strand which inspires many social democrats.

It is also a feature of the communitarian view which will be resisted by those who subscribe to fashionable ideas of 'the end of politics'. Yet the intensely politically contested character of policy on education and the family should persuade us that politics has not ended, and cannot be ended by the liberal legalist attempt to resolve such disputed issues by the entrenchment and interpretation of rights.

The most incongruous implication of local justice for conventional liberals, however, is that fairness makes conflicting demands on us. Sometimes we cannot avoid injustice. There is a sort of endemic moral scarcity which runs parallel with the finitude of resources. This is an implication – in my view a reality – that is deeply at odds with our inherited traditions of moral and political thinking. Talk of trade-offs and costs and benefits trivialises the fact that public policy inescapably involves making hard collective choices among genuine goods. Both welfare reform and tax reform encompass such choices. The distributional conflicts such choices entail are better understood in terms of the conflicting demands of fairness. Some of these conflicts concern intergenerational fairness – an issue I cannot discuss here, except in passing, despite its clear and growing importance. All of them can be resolved only by collective choices whose proper sphere is that of political practice, not courts of law.[16] And these are not policy decisions which can be settled by appeal to the doctrines of political economy, but political choices informed by ethical judgments.

The demands of fairness are most urgent in the central issue of the post-social-democratic period: that of developing a policy for livelihood when the post-war pursuit of full employment is no longer realistic. Conventional social-democratic thought has relied upon ambitious reskilling programmes with a resumption of rapid economic growth. But today incessant change in the division of labour arising from new information technologies is imposing on us not only recurrent changes of job but also changes of occupation.[17] In an age of unceasing technological innovation, a poor education system guarantees economic failure. The idea that British economic culture can be renewed without fundamental reform of education is plainly an exercise in fantasy. In all these respects, the current social-democratic emphasis on reskilling is entirely appropriate.

At the same time, it goes against all experience to

suppose that even lifetime reskilling programmes can move us back to something akin to full employment. 'Full employment' looks like a policy designed for stabler times, in which occupations were less ephemeral, the division of labour in less of a flux, and the institution of job-holding itself more secure. Moreover the confidence that higher rates of economic growth, even if sustained, will more than dent the rising underlying rates of long-term unemployment has little in post-war history to support it. No matter how it is measured, economic activity has increased enormously during that period. At least since the early 1970s, that expansion has not prevented the core rate of unemployment moving steadily upwards. In this respect over-reliance on economic growth as a comprehensive solution for our social dilemmas is seriously misguided.

No successor to the social-democratic settlement is morally tolerable, or in the long term politically sustainable, which does not contain a credible and meaningful alternative to full-employment policy. Even if it has allowed somewhat lower levels of joblessness than our European partners, neoliberal deregulation of the labour market in Britain has been accompanied by a growth in inequality and associated with mobility pathologies. These include marital breakdown, which is commonest in places where labour mobility is high and unemployment high.[18] We must therefore, look at radical alternatives, however unpromising they may be in immediate fiscal terms. One alternative recognises that the institution of the job itself is likely to decline in future. This view, developed most ambitiously by Jeremy Rifkin,[19] sees our inherited culture of work as itself becoming increasingly obsolescent because of technology-driven economic change. Its policy implication is some form of Basic Income scheme.[20]

Another view, advocated powerfully by Frank Field MP,[21] favours a state-supervised scheme of compulsory insurance against employment risk (and to fund pensions). Unlike the present National Insurance sham, contributions would remain the property of individuals. Interestingly, both of these alternatives avoid the moral hazards of means-tested, or targeted[22] benefits, and the neoliberal dependency culture they produce. No less significantly, they each address the interest in autonomy, the strengthening of which was another of the unintended consequences of the 1980s.

My concern here is to insist that the political choices we make about these schemes are ethical and political and not primarily economic or fiscal. There are powerful ethical arguments against the Basic Income approach which give strong support to a policy of self-provision in many areas of welfare. Basic Income schemes may be exclusionary because they attach extra significance to citizenship and because the political incentive to reintegrate the excluded may be diminished if they are guaranteed a tolerable minimum. Only in late-industrial cultures can deskilling occur; in pre-industrial societies poised on the edge of subsistence and early industrialism not yet rich enough to afford well-developed welfare states, it is an impossibility. For the foreseeable future, however, there is every prospect that a growing proportion of the population will be marginalised, and kept on a miserable subsistence by the growing productivity of the dwindling working population. A Basic Income scheme could only enhance this risk, since it would make it easier for society to abandon excluded groups with a clear conscience.

The other crucial objection to Basic Income schemes is that they institutionalise the lack of reciprocal obligation. As they are unconditional guarantees of subsistence, Basic or Citizen's Income schemes strengthen the culture of liberty without responsibility, of individual choice without corresponding obligation, which is the least benign moral inheritance of individualism. They reinforce the denial of agency and the lack of mutuality and a sense of membership which are the most disabling features of the culture of dependency of the so-called 'underclass'.

The decisive objections to Basic Income schemes are therefore not fiscal but ethical. (Such schemes might well be cheaper than workfare, which may account for the interest which the newer New Right is taking in them.[23]) They take no account of British people's continuing attachment to the idea of deserts in the common culture of norms of fairness. Indeed they run counter to the common moral intuition that an unconditional guarantee of subsistence income, regardless of need or merit, is undeserved. They override the shared social understanding of the relationship of subsistence with work. And they go against the grain of much in our moral culture which affirms that for able-bodied people, welfare rights are properly conditional on the discharge of public duties. For all these reasons, Basic Income schemes are no antidote to the culture of dutiless individualism we inherit from the neoliberal experiment.[24] Insofar as social democrats endorse such schemes, they show they now seek only to cure or palliate the evils of economic individualism by extending the culture of unconditional individual rights within welfare institutions. In most areas of welfare policy, however, the common life is served by attaching duties to rights.

These ethical considerations lead me to the conclusion that, whereas welfare reform cannot be the application of any single principle, it should not on the whole go down the Basic Income road. Instead it must seek to create the conditions for self-provision for all who are capable of making a productive contribution to society.[25] A sharp and clear distinction needs to be made between contexts in which participation in common institutions is vital to social cohesion – contexts such as schooling and healthcare – and other contexts, such as pension provision, in which the aim of policy is the prevention of poverty and dependency. It is in these areas of the welfare state that new institutions are needed which foster independence and promote self-provision. The ethical basis of self-provision is not the neoliberal ideal of individual choice, but rather the communitarian conception of the reciprocity of rights and obligations. Late-industrial societies such as ours, face the problem of growth in unemployment and poverty rooted in deskilling and family breakdown. In accepting the conclusion that the future of welfare institutions lies with new forms of self-provision, we are acknowledging that there is no quick fix. A new policy agenda on work and the family, replacing the post-war social-democratic policy of full employment, cannot promise rapid results or easy solutions. It must confront the evident truths that the growth of an excluded underclass can only be slowed, let alone reversed, by radical reforms in education and in welfare. Reinstating conceptions of meritocratic selection and making rights to public assistance conditional on obligations to participate in reskilling programmes, may prove indigestible to many British social democrats.[26]

Any workable reform of welfare must begin from the fact that the Beveridge settlement has been destroyed not only by neoliberal policy but also by the vast changes in family life and in the labour market that have occurred over the past half century. The changed economic situation of women in particular makes any attempt at reconstituting Beveridge undesirable as well as unfeasible. Whatever their structure, welfare institutions in future must be minimally paternalist, and friendly to diversity in forms of family life. It would be a fundamental mistake for communitarians to follow the social engineers of the Right or the Left,[27] in viewing welfare policy as a device for the preservation or revival of 'the traditional family'. Its primary role in a liberal society is not to promote or protect any particular form of family life. Instead policy should enhance individual competences – the control over their time and working conditions people need if they are to form families of any enduring kinds – and so facilitate the formation of lasting personal relationships.

The view of welfare policy as an instrument for re-engineering forms of long eroded family life is mistaken for another reason. Today's Britain, unlike Beveridge's, harbours a considerable measure of cultural diversity, which policy must respect. Recent immigrant communities, in all their own diversity, do not necessarily elevate autonomy over all other human interests, or revere it as an ideal. A welfare and social policy which aims to enhance individual autonomy cannot in such a multicultural setting be designed to secure the proliferation of liberal individuals. That would be a policy of liberal cultural imperialism, an assimilationist programme to impose the liberal ideal of autonomy on diverse communities. Public policy in a pluralist state which respects these traditions and communities rightly protects autonomous choice of exit from them. We cannot restore a seamless monoculture animated by the liberal ideal of autonomy.[28]

Our inherited welfare institutions and policies need radical revision now that the paternalism and cultural consensus which the Beveridge settlement expressed are unworkable and unacceptable. Economic change has rendered earlier family forms unsustainable and indeed redundant. Moreover, moral beliefs in the 'traditional family' are vanishingly remote from the lives of the great majority of the population. They cannot be revived by any political project, whether traditionalist-conservative or ethical-socialist in content. Yet welfare reform cannot be value-neutral, a vain search for a technical fix for poverty. The principal causes of most modern poverty are cultural and are not removed by the provision of income.[29] Nor can public policy be indifferent to the ways in which families are formed and dissolved. It is wholly wrong to penalise or scapegoat single parents. But it cannot be irrelevant to policy that single parenthood is only rarely a chosen condition. Concern for individual wellbeing is not shown by policies which treat one-parent families as if they were always, or even typically, expressions of autonomous choices. In a liberal culture in which autonomy is for most people vital to wellbeing, neither familial fundamentalism nor liberal neutrality is an intelligent response to the fragility of families. The goal of policy should be to enhance individual competences, to ensure that the obligations of parenthood are understood and accepted, and to assist single parents to return, or sometimes, to enter for the first time, the world of productive work, because participation in it is, for us, the precondition of self-esteem and independence.

In all these areas of policy, the aim is to contain the centripetal forces of market individualism so as to reconcile them with the renewal of common life. Communitarian liberalism seeks to achieve this by linking the distribution of particular goods with shared understandings of need, merit and deserts, as these are found in the common culture. It emphasises that only collective choice can resolve conflicts arising from the conflicting claims of local justice. Such choices can only be political, informed by ethical considerations which track the complex and sometimes conflicting demands of fairness. They aim to reconcile these demands not by invoking any 'theory of justice' but by articulating a common understanding of the sort of society we wish to live in. In so doing they express the key insight of the communitarian liberal perspective – that human lives conducted within a public culture that is desolated and fractured are impoverished no matter how many individual choices they contain.

What we can hope for

For us, individualism is an historical fate, which we can hope to temper, but not to overcome. Against both the newer forms of the New Right project and conservative forms of communitarianism, I have argued that there is no going back to the old moral world we have lost, even if such a reversion were desirable. The unintended cultural consequence of neoliberal policy was to accelerate all the inherent tendencies in late modern societies to deplete the common moral culture. Apart from the ephemeral episode of neoliberalism, the relationship between the permanent revolution of the global market and inherited forms of family and social life is not one of easy coexistence or stable equilibrium. It is one of inherent tension and endemic instability.[30] Individualist market institutions of the sort we inherited in Britain detach individuals from localities and communities and weaken commitments to families. They do this by imposing unending mobility on people and by routinising high levels of economic risk, so that all relationships come to be perceived as revocable and transitory.

Our inherited individualist economic and moral cultures will be defended by unreflective economic liberals, or those for whom repressive communities are still living memories, who promote individual autonomy. My argument here, however, is that an anomically individualist society, such as ours has become, does not act to strengthen autonomy. That depends on the existence of a strong public culture, rich in options, and embodied in common institutions. Moreover, autonomy is only one human interest, one component in individual wellbeing, even in a society such as ours; the satisfaction of needs for belonging and for stable relationships and attachments, is equally essential to our flourishing as individuals. How, then, might the incorrigible individualism of a late liberal culture such as Britain's be moderated and contained by common institutions?

The human needs which traditional social forms may once have met have not diminished in importance merely because conservatives no longer take much interest in them. Against rights-based liberalism and social democracy, I have argued that the extension of a culture of rights, necessary as it may be in some areas of policy, is no antidote to the asocial individualism that is our chief danger. The liberal conception of a state that is neutral on all issues to do with the good life is not realisable in practice. Or if it is, it can only be short-lived, and at the expense of the liberal culture it properly exists to renew. A state committed to renewing a liberal culture cannot be indifferent to the fate of institutions and forms of common life on which such a culture depends for its survival. I have argued that both social-democratic ideas of equality and neoliberal ideas of unrestricted market freedom, cut against the grain of deeply held popular sentiments of fairness, in which notions of merit, deserts and need are central. Only by respecting these sentiments can public policy hope to be effective. In the wake of social democracy policy should aim at local justice, the balancing of irreconcilable claims within complex fairness.

It is not reasonable to hope to put the social-democratic project back on the road. That belonged within an historical niche that is gone beyond hope of recovery. Nor will there be any renaissance of collectivist sentiment arising from the failures of neoliberal individualism.[31] To imagine otherwise is to misread entirely the lessons of the 1980s, which showed the overwhelming power and urgency within our culture of the demand for individual autonomy. If we are humbler in our hopes, we will no more return to the collectivist dreams of the past than we will strive to resurrect the vanished folkways of earlier generations. We will seek ways to make our economic culture more friendly to the needs of the people it exists to serve. We will aim to contrive institutions and policies which moderate its risks for them, and which make it easier for them to reconcile in their lives the need for enduring relationships with the imperatives of economic survival. We will seek to make the distribution of skills and opportunities fairer. In this way we can hope to make our individualism less possessive and more convivial.

No single policy reform can be a panacea for our economic culture. Many of the ills of our society can only be cured slowly and in part, since they arise from sources in our culture which governments can certainly aggravate by their policies, but over which their leverage is otherwise strictly limited. Our economic life is only an aspect of our flawed and fractured late-modern culture.[32] Yet unless they are reformed so as to make their workings more humanly tolerable, liberal market institutions will lose political legitimacy. This is no small point, since it is an implication of the communitarian liberal view that, for us, as inheritors of a late-modern individualist culture, there is no sustainable alternative to the institutions of liberal capitalism, however reformed.

The first duty of political thought is to understand the present. The danger of the new social-democratic consensus is that it tracks a world which has now disappeared irretrievably. Would it not be another of history's ironies if we were to rid ourselves of the errors of the 1980s without perceiving that, in concert with the silent forces that shape events, they have transformed our world irreversibly?

58

Notes

1. For political statements of conservative communitarianism, see Harris, R., 1992, *The conservative community*, London, Centre for Policy Studies, and Willetts, D., 1993, *Civic conservatism*, London, Social Market Foundation. For a Left version of conservative communitarianism, see Dennis, N., and Halsey, A.H., *English ethical socialism*, Oxford, Oxford University Press. The elements of a liberal communitarianism are, I believe, to be found in the writings of Isaiah Berlin and Joseph Raz. See Gray, J., 1995, *Berlin*, London and Princeton, N.J.: Harper/Collins (Fontana Modern Master) and Raz, J., 1986, *The morality of freedom*, Oxford, Clarendon Press.

2. See Gray, J., 1995, *Enlightenment's wake: politics and culture at the close of the modern age*, London, Routledge; ch. 10-12.

3. Compelling statements of this view are Lester, A., 'Can we achieve a new constitutional settlement?' in Crouch, C., and Marquand, D., eds., 1995, *Reinventing collective action*, Oxford, Blackwell; Barnett, A., 1995, *The defining moment: prospects for a new Britain under Labour*, London, Charter 88; and Wright, T., and Marquand, D., 'Come the revolution', *The Guardian*, 23 October 1995.

4. *The Times*, 20 July 1995.

5. In a later article, Rees-Mogg endorses a sort of cyberspace anarchy as an alternative to any kind of national government. See *The Times*, 31 August 1995. It is difficult to see how this wild dystopia can be described as any kind of conservative vision; but it is typical of a certain kind of conservative thought today.

6. Gray, J., 1993, *The post-communist societies in transition: a social market perspective*, London, Social Market Foundation; republished as chapter five of

Enlightenment's wake: politics and culture at the close of the modern age, London, Routledge, 1995.

7. Goodhart, D., 1994, *The reshaping of the German social market*, London, Institute for Public Policy Research; 37.

8. Hutton, W., 1995, *The state we're in*, London, Jonathan Cape. This does not mean that we cannot make useful borrowings and adaptations from other economic cultures, as Will Hutton has argued in his important and illuminating book.

9. For a compelling statement of one such post-federalist European project, see Goldsmith, Sir J., 1995, *The trap and the response*, London, Macmillan.

10. This is true of the Borrie report of the commission on *Social justice*, of the Dahrendorf report on *Wealth creation and social cohesion in a free society*, and of Patricia Hewitt's notable T.H. Marshall Memorial Lecture 'Social justice in a global economy?'.

11. Gray, J., 1993, *Beyond the New Right*, London and New York, Routledge; 76-92.

12. Raz, J., 1986, *The morality of freedom*, Oxford, Clarendon Press. I remain indebted to the author's critique of libertarian, rights-based and egalitarian political moralities. However I think that context-specific principles of fairness are necessary in many areas. These are the ones where human needs are not satiable but are yet basic, where they are satiable but cannot all be met, and, perhaps most fundamentally, where the criteria of satiability itself cannot avoid mention of norms of fairness.

13. By contrast, *The Economist* has argued ('The myth of the powerless state', 7 October 1995) that 'global integration has left government with about as many economic powers as they ever had'. This may be true. But as *The Economist* recognises elsewhere in the same article, the effect of global integration has been to alter the consequences of using these powers, and thereby to impose new constraints on their uses. It can be argued that the impact of economic globalisation (in its various manifestations) on the macroeconomic policies of sovereign states has been exaggerated; it is silly to suggest that the costs of certain policy options have not greatly increased as a consequence of globalisation, increased so much indeed, as to remove them from the political agenda.

14. Walzer, M., 1983, *Spheres of justice*, New York, Basic Books. Also, Elster, J., 1992, *Local justice*, Cambridge, Cambridge University Press.

15. Wooldridge, A., 1995, *Meritocracy and the classless society*, London, Social Market Foundation and Pollard, S., 1995, *Schools, selection and the Left*, London, Social Market Foundation. It may be worth noting that support for meritocratic practices in educational contexts does not commit one to the view that society as a whole should be reordered according to a comprehensive meritocratic conception of justice. That conception has been destroyed by critics as different as Hayek and Michael Young. Nor, of course, does such support entail that meritocratic criteria are the only ones relevant in all educational contexts. It is obvious that special needs and disabilities may also be salient.

16. This does not imply any opposition on my part to welfare rights. On the contrary, I support them, but as alterable artefacts of legislation, not as derivations from illusory 'theories of justice'. See Gray, J., 1993, *Beyond the New Right*; 99-110.

17. I am well aware that on available evidence the extent of the growth of job insecurity remains somewhat controversial. See on this *Income data services focus, Quarterly 74*, March 1995, 'The jobs mythology'. What is less controversial is the expectation that job security will decline in future, and with it our inherited culture of work which presupposes job-holding as its central institution.

18. An example of such a place in Britain may be Swindon, which is currently the subject of a research project being conducted by Matthew D'Ancona.

19. Rifkin, J., 1995 *The end of work: the decline of the global labour force and the dawn of the post-market era*, New York, G.P. Putnam's Sons.

20. Various schemes are discussed in the *Citizens's income bulletin*, particularly Nos. 18 (July 1994), 19 (February 1995) and 20 (July 1995).

21. A comprehensive statement of Frank Field's proposals can be found in Field, F., 1995, *Making welfare work: reconstructing welfare for the millennium*, London, Institute of Community Studies.

22. Not all forms of targeting involve means-testing. Some involve categorisation by other factors such as age or disability, and do not necessarily carry the moral hazards of means-testing. A comprehensive welfare reform of the sort we undoubtedly need must recognise that different forms of allocation of benefits are appropriate, depending on the shared social understanding of the goods concerned, and on the consequences of their mode of allocation. Pluralism is unavoidable here too.

23. For a New Right defence of a Basic Income, see Duncan, A., and Hobson, D., 1995, *Saturn's children*, London, Sinclair Stevens.

24. It may be that limited and conditional Basic Income schemes have an important role in any policy aiming to protect the human interests once promoted by full employment policy. I do not discuss this possibility, since I am concerned to assess Basic Income schemes in their most distinctive and radical form.

25. Of course, some welfare rights are properly recognised to be unconditional, or, more precisely, to be owed independently of contribution to society. The welfare rights created by some disabilities may fall into this category. There is no single ethical justification for all forms of legitimate welfare provision.

26. Obligations to accept reskilling were a key element in the immensely successful Swedish pro-active labour policy, which still repays study despite its collapse along with much else in the Swedish social-democratic model.

27. For a nostalgist Left version of familial fundamentalism, whose implication for welfare policy is large-scale social engineering, see Dennis, N., and Erdos, G., 1993, foreword by Halsey, A.H., *Families without fatherhood,* London, Institute for Economic Affairs, Health and Welfare Unit, *Choice in welfare series no 12.*

28. I am aware that this is a great simplification of complex issues. For a helpful critique of standard liberal views on multiculturalism, see Parekh, B., 'Superior people: the narrowness of liberalism from Mill to Rawls', *Times Literary Supplement,* 25 February 1994. See also, Raz, J., 1994, 'Multiculturalism: a liberal perspective', in his book, *Ethics in the public domain,* Oxford, Clarendon Press.

29. Gray, J., 1989, *Limited government: a positive agenda,* London, Institute for Economic Affairs. Reprinted as chapter one of Gray, J., 1993, *Beyond the New Right,* London, Routledge; 33-4.

30. This is a point not sufficiently acknowledged in Fukuyama, F., 1995, *Trust: the social virtues and the creation of prosperity,* London, Hamish Hamilton.

31. This is the hope of several contributors to Crouch, C., and Marquand, D., 1995, eds., *Reinventing collective action,* Oxford, Blackwell.

32. Gray, J., 1995, *Enlightenment's wake: politics and culture at the close of the modern age,* London, Routledge.